DAILY
CONTEMPLATIONS
for
MISFIT
CHRISTIANS

1

Elane O'Rourke & Benton Stokes

ADVENT + CHRISTMAS

ELANE O'ROURKE is a spiritual mentor, teacher, and researcher, with years of pastoring and professoring informing her worldview. She specializes in making sense of difficult ideas and listening for what the Spirit is doing in your life.

BENTON STOKES is a worship leader, songwriter and recording artist whose songs are spiritually intelligent and emotionally relevant. As our Resident Creative he specializes in real life, intimate prayer, and making the ordinary beautiful.

OUR PEOPLE ARE smart, curious, post-evangelical, progressive, agnostic, creative, eloquent, awkward, LGBTQ+ and justice-allied. We are sex-positive, body-positive, spirit-positive and Spirit-positive.

WE CREATED SCHOOL FOR SEEKERS in 2014 to give Christian misfits—usually former evangelicals and political liberals—a place to heal and grow in their relationships with themselves, God, and others.

WE EXPLORE SPIRITUAL LIFE through a wide-angle Trinitarian lens, starting from one truth: God loves and accepts us all and desires relationship with each of us.

WE COMPANION through programs like *17 Embraceable Ideas (that will reconstruct your faith and transform your life)* and *Reading The Bible As If It Matters*, along with life-affirming spiritual direction and coaching.

OUR PODCAST is *Cocktail Theology*, where we talk about life, God, sex, religion, music, roller coasters (both physical and emotional), and anything else that matters, with no filters. We also enjoy a cocktail while we chat (like most of our listeners). You can find it wherever you listen to podcasts.

You could read each day's entry while stopped at a red light, or waiting in line, or bored at work. We don't recommend that approach.

If you want to grow, or heal, or know God and yourself better, this is what we suggest.

Schedule 15 minutes each day. Put it on your calendar. Set an alarm if you need to.

Have a journal and a pen at hand. Physically writing your responses stimulates your brain to retain the ideas and begins to create the new neural pathways that can lead to change.

You may want to light a candle or make a cup of tea. Take in the scent, warmth, taste, sounds; keep engaging your body and mind together.

Begin with 3 deep breaths, followed by a set prayer (see next page for some possibilities).

Following each reflection is a thought question or a prayer suggestion or a practice. Take 5-10 minutes to write in your journal: answer the questions, rewrite the prayer, make a plan to try the practice.

If you find the reflection challenging, try not to argue with it. Instead, try on the ideas that bother you, asking "how would my life be different if I believed this?"

Close with that day's prayer, or a set prayer, or a free prayer of your own.

Take 3 more deep breaths.

Repeat daily.

SOME SET PRAYERS

MORNING

I will sing of your strength in the morning; I will sing of your love, You are my fortress, my refuge in times of trouble. O my Strength, I sing praise to you, O loving God.

Holy and everlasting Father, thank you for bringing me to this new day. Preserve me with your mighty power, that I may not fall into sin, or be overcome by adversity, and in all I do direct me toward the fulfillment of your Kingdom, through Jesus Christ my Lord (*or, through the power of your holy names*), Amen.

EVENING

O God, thank you for the blessings of the day that is past. Bring me and those I love safely to the morning hours so we may rise and enjoy your presence again. Amen.

O gracious light, pure brightness of the everliving Father in heaven, O Jesus Christ, holy and blessed! As we come now to the setting of the sun, and our eyes behold the vesper light, we sing your praises, O God: Father, Son, and Holy Spirit. You are worthy at all times to be praised by happy voices, O Son of God, O Giver of life, and to be glorified through all the worlds.

ANYTIME

Oh Lord, open my lips and my mouth shall declare your praise. Praise Father, Son, and Holy Spirit, both now and forever. The God who was, who is, and is to come at the end of the ages.

HOPE

ADVENT WEEK 1

FIRST SUNDAY

In the beginning was the Word, and the Word was with God, and the Word was God. He was in the beginning with God. All things came into being through him, and without him not one thing came into being. What has come into being in him was life, and the life was the light of all people. The light shines in the darkness, and the darkness did not overcome it. —John 1:1-5

If you're in the northern hemisphere, the hours of light are growing fewer and dimmer. Night begins earlier and ends later, with darkness that is thick and dense.

Today begins the season of Advent. It makes sense that these four weeks before Christmas would be shrouded in darkness (so if you're in Australia you might want to flip your Christian calendar around to start at the end of May...). The season is about waiting and preparing for the coming of the light of the world. It is so much easier to recognize our spiritual darkness when the material world is dark too.

The traditional symbol of this season is the ring of Advent candles, symbolizing the cycle of the year and the neverendingness of eternity. On the first Sunday (and every night after if we remember) we light one candle. As the nights get progressively longer and the Advent weeks pass we light more. Their light increases each week, expanding into the darker-and-darker-still.

Tonight's tiny flame will pierce the gloom, including the gloom in our hearts, if we let it. The name of the first candle is Hope, because it is the coming of the Light of the World that provides us mortals the hope of the Eternal One.

—EOR

What simple action can you take each day of Advent to summon light and hope, for yourself or others?

FIRST MONDAY

A king is not saved by his great army; a warrior is not delivered by his great strength... Truly the eye of the Lord is on those who are in awe of him, on those who hope in his steadfast love, to deliver their soul from death, and to keep them alive in famine. Our soul waits for the Lord... Let your steadfast love, O Lord, be upon us, even as we hope in you.
—Psalm 33:13-22, excerpted

There are days, even months and years, when having hope can be difficult.

Maybe you've suffered a loss: lost your job, said goodbye to your partner or spouse, watched a child die.

Maybe you've been reading the news, or listening to your permanently pessimistic sibling, and the world seems irrevocably broken.

Maybe you're ill, suffering from a condition or waiting for a diagnosis.

Or maybe you're facing a decision that terrifies you, even though you know it needs to be made.

We all have those seasons, when hope seems farther away than the limits of the universe. Reaching for hope can seem like a waste of time and energy.

Here's the thing: if your hope depends upon specific people, or on your circumstances, or on an election or choice or system, you will lose hope, because people will let you down at some point, your circumstances will be bad sometimes, and you will be disappointed.

The only reason hope can "spring eternal" is because God is eternal, and it is from trusting God that we can gain hope.

Hope is possible because it is grounded on the neverending, never breaking, always and forever love of God.

The eye of God is on those who are in awe of him, the Psalmist tells us. Their hearts are glad, even in the midst of sorrow, because they trust in God's steadfast love.

When hope seems far away, write down seven good things that have happened in your life. Then meditate on the fact that all that good is a window into God's impossibly permanent love for you.

—EOR

When you have lost hope, even for a moment, what was the disappointment that prompted that loss?

FIRST TUESDAY

————

For God alone my soul waits in silence, for my hope is from God. —Psalm 62:5

Some ancient Greeks speculated that the original model for humans had been divided into two persons, each seeking the other to unite their souls and once again become whole.

I grew up thinking that somewhere out there was my soulmate—my other half—and when I found them "the two shall become one" (to use the biblical phrase). Usually when we use the term "soulmate" we are talking about the object of our romantic affection. While I've had lovers and spouses and good friends with whom I felt fully at ease and known, I can't say I've ever noticed the other half of myself across the table, or shopping at Target.

If your hope for wholeness relies upon the right romantic partner, listen up: you are already whole. And: even the very best humans will fail from time to time, no matter how special they seem in that first flush of hormonal happiness.

Your soul *is* reaching out for connection. If you're looking for a human being, your soul's hope will be pinned to that person. Being a soulmate is a lot of responsibility to put on a mere mortal.

When you come to *know* God, and not just know *about* God, then you have met the true mate of your soul.

Knowing God is about intimacy, the kind of relationship you get through lots of talking, listening, and just hanging out with someone.

Practice pouring out your heart to God and inviting God into your holiday preparations. Let God be your companion as well as your refuge. Your soul will be fully at ease and known when it is in the presence of its true soulmate, our beloved God.

—EOR

A prayer to try when words don't come easily.
Feel free to revise to fit your own voice.

Oh, mate of my soul, teach me to long for your companionship. Help me to crave your presence as I do the company of a lover. You are my rock and my refuge in times of trouble; be my hope and joy in times of celebration as well.

FIRST WEDNESDAY

Gone is my glory, and all that I had hoped for from the Lord…. My soul continually thinks of it and is bowed down within me. But this I call to mind, and therefore I have hope: The steadfast love of the Lord never ceases, God's mercies never come to an end... The Lord is my portion, says my soul, therefore I will hope in God. — Lamentations 3:17-21

Do you always get the credit and the recognition you deserve? How about all the benefits to which you feel entitled?

Are you treated with equity and respect? Or does your gender, race, age, ableness or some other marker expose you to ill treatment?

Even if you receive social privileges and don't have to deal with injustice, just living among other people means your feelings will be hurt.

That isn't trivial: we are emotional creatures, and hurt feelings matter. The Psalmist puts it this way: Gone is my glory, and all that I had hoped for from the Lord.

It takes mental and physical effort to lift our souls when they are bowed down. It's not easy to rouse ourselves and to regain hope. And if you face systemic challenges, you can feel there are no safe where can simply rest and be at home.

When your emotions are afflicted, and you feel spiritually (or physically) homeless, you might call this to mind: God's active care for you renews itself continually.

When you feel put down or shoved away, remind yourself: God is always faithful. God never rejects me, never undervalues me.

Tell your soul that it's going to be okay. Literally speak back to the deeply hidden self inside you: I see you. You are hurting. You will be okay. Though you don't believe it now, you already are okay, because you are cherished and appreciated by the One who knows you best. Not just loved by me, but by God, whose love never ceases.

—EOR

What does your soul need to hear from you today?

FIRST THURSDAY

"Here is my servant, whom I have chosen, my beloved, with whom my soul is well pleased. I will put my Spirit upon him and he will proclaim justice to the nations."
—Matthew 12:15-18a

What pleases a soul? Your soul is a hungry thing. It seeks sustenance, but it latches onto whatever it is given.

For a while your soul may settle for trashy tv or the closest body available. If you've ever depended on "casual" sex or struggled with compulsive eating, you know what a starving soul feels like, and just how short a time physical panaceas last.

Just as your body prefers nutritious food to junk, so does your soul prefer nourishment over quick fixes and cynical triumphs. Your soul may get a thrill from drama, but it thrives when it is fed consistent gentleness and kindness.

You can give it some of that by treating yourself with curiosity and care, but your soul is eternal, and only an eternal connection will satisfy your soul.

Your soul is hungry for deep connection with God, and God wants to nourish your soul. Intimacy between you and God is soul food, for you and for God, if Isaiah got that right.

Did you notice that in the scripture? God's soul was pleased. God gets something out of intimacy with you.

When you draw close to a person and build a relationship, that person can trust you with more of themselves.

When God trusts another person, God can give them more Spirit-power. We can see that with Jesus.

With God empowering you through the Spirit, you can do more of what Jesus did, like heal (yourself and others), proclaim justice, love kindness, serve well, and please your own soul.

—EOR

When have you felt strength to do something you could not have otherwise done? How did you feel?

An Advent prayer to try

Mysterious God, thank you for coming, and staying. In this Advent season, when we prepare for your arrival, may we make a suitable place in our hearts for you to dwell, now and forever.

Amen.

FIRST FRIDAY

We boast in our sufferings, knowing that suffering produces endurance, and endurance produces character, and character produces hope, and hope does not disappoint us.
—Romans 5:3-5

I've always been physically strong, so when my back finally succumbed to years of abuse it was a hard blow to both my habits and my ego. I'll leave chiro sore and tired and so emotionally drained that I have to take a minute before I drive. Self-image and fatigue and ancient fears and demon voices torture in ways the pain itself never could.

The pain is in my body but the suffering is in my head.

So I get help from therapy (both physical and mental) and from other people. Asking others for help is hard, even when I'm paying, but I'm learning to do it.

I handle it better now than I would have when I was younger, when every weakness was humiliating. Years of living through loss, and choosing how to respond, have turned humiliation into humility, and humility into hope.

Humility is the ability to claim both your strengths and weaknesses without judgment.

Hope is knowing, from experience, that this moment of suffering will pass, and anticipating the better that is next.

I'm not great at humility yet. Some days I'm ashamed of needing help and afraid of losing love.

Shame and fear will destroy you if you let them.

I can't always avoid shame and fear, but I can consistently acknowledge that God keeps pulling me through. God responds to my pleas even when I don't know I'm praying them. Choosing to recognize that reality shores up my hope, even on the bad days.

The Apostle Paul went so far as to say he boasted — took pride in — his suffering, because through suffering he gained endurance, character, and hope. I think he goes a little overboard there. I'm not spiritually advanced enough to take pride in how much I've suffered.

I think I'd happily give up suffering, tossing it into the dumpster along with the spoiled milk, even if I had to give up a little endurance too.

I wouldn't hand over hope.

—EOR

When your heart is hurting and shame and fear are not far away, how do you re-find hope?

FIRST SATURDAY

God gave me, to present to you, the word of God in its
fullness—the mystery that has been kept hidden for ages
and generations...: Christ in you, the hope of glory.
—Colossians 1:25-27

This season of the Christian calendar is about
expectation. For four weeks, today is less real
than tomorrow, since today is spent preparing
for a another day: the feast of the Incarnation,
aka Christmas.

"Christmas" is something we understand. It's a
baby born to a young girl in a strange town.
There's a star involved, and some shepherds.
Maybe gifts and a tree. We expect to feel a
certain way, and whether we wind up feeling
that way or not, we understand what it is we
are expecting.

Add in that the girl was a virgin, and that a
king was ticked off. Throw in prophecies and
angels, and still we understand what we're all
talking about.

Does anyone truly understand the Incarnation?
Take out the girl and the carols, the ornaments
and the sheep. What's left is in no way
understandable: God came to the earth in flesh
and blood, yet never left eternity. When God
departed, God remained present to us. And not
only to us, but in us.

Every Christmas we hear the story and we nod
agreeably, knowing how it turns out. But
beyond the story is God's great mystery: the

glorious hope for Jews and Gentiles, for all of creation, is Christ in us.

Our hope is not in the life after this one. Our hope is that in this life, Christ chooses to abide in and among us.

—EOR

What would it look like for you to live with hope, in expectation of what is already so, that God is here, in you?

PEACE

ADVENT WEEK 2

And let the peace of Christ rule in your hearts, to which indeed you were called in the one body. And be thankful.
—Colossians 3:15

A few weeks before he died, my deeply loved teacher stood before the hundreds who had come to hear him speak, and pronounced a blessing. I had heard it a thousand times, and spoken it myself dozens more, but that day I heard it for the first time because he said it over us.

We don't bless each other much. There's "bless you" when someone sneezes. People will say they're blessed when they want to attribute their good fortune to someone other than themselves. But lovingly, tenderly, invoke God's grace and mercy upon someone else, in their presence? Not so often.

When my teacher, who knew he would die soon, blessed us, he was thanking God and trusting God to grant us peace.

The world is not a peaceful place. The holiday season is often filled with noise and hurry, with forgotten tasks and obligations crowding out life-giving thoughts. Even our souls, which are meant to enjoy the presence of God that is promised by the season, can be terribly restless.

God intends us to be at peace when the world is in tumult. We gain peace through blessing and effort.

The effort is choosing where to put our time and attention, selecting how we respond to the world's challenges.

The blessing? Christ, who lives in our hearts and who promised peace.

Suppose you faced someone you love, put your hands on their shoulders, and said, "may the peace of Christ rule in your heart," Suppose you trusted God to do what God has promised to do: to provide presence and peace.

With his last breath my teacher is reported to have said "thank you." Sounds like peace to me.

—EOR

Who will you bless in this season? Upon whom will you call forth God's peace?

SECOND MONDAY

'Answer me when I call, O God of my right! You gave me room when I was in distress. Be gracious to me, and hear my prayer' ... When you are disturbed, do not sin; ponder it on your beds, and be silent. —Psalm 4:1, 4

God has good manners. When invited, God shows up, and on time. When we turn and close the door behind us, God does not pound on it, shouting, "you'd better let me in!"

God knows that sometimes even a loving companion is more than we can handle. Sometimes our thoughts are so loud that adding even a sweet voice to the clamor will send us over the edge. In those times, God waits; patience doesn't seem to be a problem for God.

To gain internal peace, humans need silence and solitude. That doesn't mean we're all introverts, or that silence and solitude are necessarily comfortable. Being alone with your thoughts can be terrifying, until their unruly voices hear your "hush!"

When you want sympathetic company with other people, including God, that's great. But many times—especially when you're anxious and want to be seen and noticed by someone—what our souls and minds truly need is to have room.

When we have chosen to be alone and silent, we create room for our minds to wander until they finally quiet down and stand still.

When your soul is disturbed, your first instinct may be to act, to just do something— anything—to make yourself feel better.

It may be that what your soul needs is for you to go to your room and be still, allowing the anxiety to peak in safety, and to pass.

When we give ourselves a little space, and some quiet, it's much easier to trust in God. When we deeply trust in God, we can rest and sleep in peace.

—EOR

A prayer for getting through anxiety

Oh, God who graciously waits and listens, you are trustworthy. You do not lie, or make false promises. I'm struggling. My mind is overwhelmed with details and decisions. I'm worrying, and fearful, and feel like I'm going to burst from my skin. Help me to find a quiet place where I can be alone, and safe, and hear your sweet gentle voice giving me peace. Amen.

SECOND TUESDAY

Let me hear what God the Lord will speak, for he will speak peace... to those who turn to him in their hearts... Steadfast love and faithfulness will meet; righteousness and peace will kiss each other.   —Psalm 85:8,10

When I was around 8 I was spending my long school break with family friends who lived in Texas. He was a Pentecostal preacher with a cheerful face and piercing eyes. She was always dressed simply and appropriately, her hair pulled up into a bun. Except for Sundays, when she attached extra hair—a "fall" it was called then—to plump up the bun and add curls. They were warm and welcoming people. Unlike my tiny family, they and their four children were loud.

One night the preacher and his wife got into a disagreement in the kitchen. The girls' room, where I was staying, was just down the hall. I wasn't used to voices in the night, much less to bickering voices breaking the peace, so the sound woke me and sent me into the kitchen where I commanded my host and hostess to lower their voices because people were trying to sleep.

"Cheeky" is the word you're looking for. Two days later I went to stay with a different family friend.

If I was seeking a peaceful night I went about it the wrong way.

The voice of peace does not shout. It does not chide, or threaten, or draw undue attention to itself. The voice of peace is never pushy, nor is it anxious. And it definitely doesn't insult its hosts or condescend to anyone.

If you ever hear a voice doing those things, whether it's outside or inside your head, trust me: it's not the voice of peace. If you hear people shouting for peace, it's not peace they're looking for but justice or vindication or some other thing worth having.

The voice of peace is peace itself. The voice of peace is Christ's own voice. It is a whisper of love heard through the effort of faith.

Perhaps salvation is less an eternity in heaven than it is the experience of Christ's peace in this life

Perhaps the way to that eternal life is less about religious rightness and more about turning back toward the voice of peace, over and over again.

From the other side of Christmas, Peace whispers sweetly: I am here.

—EOR

How can you turn your attention away from the noise of daily living? What do you need today in order to hear Christ's voice?

The people who walked in darkness have seen a great light; those who lived in a land of deep darkness—on them light has shined...For all the boots of the tramping warriors and all the garments rolled in blood shall be burned as fuel for the fire. For a child has been born for us, a son given to us; authority rests upon his shoulders; and he is named Wonderful Counselor, Mighty God, Everlasting Father, Prince of Peace. —Isaiah 9:2, 5-6

Christmas celebrations differ widely even among churches. Some listen to choirs and share the Eucharist at midnight Christmas Eve. Others sing along to carols two weeks early so members can stay home on the big day.

Two traditions seem close to universal. One is the four-year-old wearing angel wings who stares blankly at the captive audience while the children's minister prompts loudly from the front row. The other is this reading from Isaiah 9.

Isaiah is proclaiming liberation, a literal release from the yoke of oppression. The child to whom he refers is Hezekiah, who restored the temple after its destruction and invited the scattered tribes of Israel to come back to Jerusalem for Passover.

Has any earthly king ever done that?

I don't think there's ever been a people who haven't walked in darkness. Internal. External. The demons within. The oppressors without.

Has there ever been a person who hasn't longed for peace? For enough? For the quieting of self-comparison? Or, simply, a tiny bit of pleasant predictability?

Each Advent we read these words from the prophet Isaiah telling us that the child born to us will be called the prince of peace, and that he has the authority to reign righteously and forever.

Each Advent, the passage also reminds us that true peace must travel from our joyful hearts into the painful world. True peace from the One Sovereign becomes real when people are set free, and we live at war no more. Inside or out.

The promise of a wonderful counselor, someone to stand by us, comfort and guide, is fulfilled by our practiced, vulnerable, relationship with God. And: we need people who step in, stand by, point, and wait.

—EOR

Where is your lack of peace this week? What deep need can only God (and counseling) begin to address?

SECOND THURSDAY

As Jesus was now approaching the path down from the
Mount of Olives, the whole multitude of the disciples began
to praise God joyfully with a loud voice for all the deeds of
power that they had seen, saying, Blessed is the king who
comes in the name of the Lord! Peace in heaven, and glory in
the highest heaven! As he came near and saw the city, he
wept over it, saying, If you, even you, had only recognized on
this day the things that make for peace!
— Luke 19:37-38, 41-42

Today's meditation and prayer will be an excerpt from
Longfellow's poem, *I Heard the Bells on Christmas Day*:

I heard the bells on Christmas Day
Their old, familiar carols play,
And wild and sweet
The words repeat
Of peace on earth, good-will to men!

Then from each black, accursed mouth
The cannon thundered in the South,
And with the sound
The carols drowned
Of peace on earth, good-will to men!

It was as if an earthquake rent
The hearth-stones of a continent,
And made forlorn
The households born
Of peace on earth, good-will to men!

And in despair I bowed my head;
"There is no peace on earth," I said:
"For hate is strong,
And mocks the song
Of peace on earth, good-will to men!"

Then pealed the bells more loud and
deep:
"God is not dead; nor doth he sleep!
The Wrong shall fail,
The Right prevail,
With peace on earth, good-will to men!"

SECOND FRIDAY

The Advocate, the Holy Spirit, whom the Father will send in my name, will teach you everything, and remind you of all that I have said to you. Peace I leave with you; my peace I give to you. I do not give to you as the world gives. Do not let your hearts be troubled, and do not let them be afraid.
—John 14:26-27

What did his disciples feel when Jesus died, returned, and then left them again?

Angry. Afraid. Abandoned.

Babies cling to their mothers (or other primary caretakers) for a reason. It's not affection: we need that adult in order to survive. The wailing only infants can manage is a biological and emotional expression of fear and abandonment. Babies don't have words; their cries emerge like a siren proclaiming danger.

Over time we gain independence, but that primal need never goes away. When a loving parent is present, besides getting our physical needs met, we feel safely connected. We can sleep,

When people we depend upon leave us, the infant inside us cries and reaches out, grasping the empty space they were in. We feel deep pain and sorrow and fear, as if both love and survival are out of reach.

We feel the opposite of peace.

Our souls are the spiritual infants of ourselves.

They reach out constantly, grabbing whatever they can, nursing on whatever we give them. What they want is their Mother, God.

When your soul is clinging to God, it rests and thrives.

I imagine the souls of Jesus' disciples were bereft. Until the Holy Spirit came, their inner infants must have grieved. They must have been confused, abandoned, and anything but peaceful.

Jesus's promise of peace is fulfilled by the presence of the Spirit. When you are aware of the Spirit's presence it is much easier to quiet your troubled mind and to release your fears.

God will not leave you alone, ever. Let that knowledge be a source of peace.

—EOR

When have you known the ache of abandonment? How have you begun to heal?

SECOND SATURDAY

Those who live according to the flesh set their minds on the things of the flesh, but those who live according to the Spirit set their minds on the things of the Spirit. To set the mind on the flesh is death, but to set the mind on the Spirit is life and peace. — Romans 8:5-6

If you've been buying presents, making lists, eating the next cookie, you may be extra aware of the physical side of mortal life. Presents, lists, cookies are all material things, and they are all good. (I am more fond of cookies than presents, myself, but a checked-off task list is a thing of beauty.)

It's a fleshly focused season, to use the Apostle Paul's word, this lead-up to Christmas. When Paul warns against the things of the flesh he's not talking about your body, or anyone else's body. Paul doesn't mean that bodies are bad, or desiring is bad, or sex/eating/drinking/dancing are bad. He would have been just fine with cookies if he'd known about them, and the Christian Bible is full of human-given gifts.

The problem with flesh is not that it's material or the object of physical desires. It's that flesh decays. It passes away, yet demands attention. The flesh distracts our eyes away from the things of the Spirit.

Television takes time away from reading. Rushed meals become a mainstay. Weighing our value by our income, rather than by our care for others, is a foundation for our society,

That doesn't mean TV and fast food and having money (or not having it) are immoral. It does mean that they are powerful seducers of our minds, and our sticky souls latch onto them with a death grip.

You are not merely matter, not a pile of chemicals or potential energy.

You are an immortal being living a material life. Both the physical and the spiritual can be life-giving, but the physical is a lot noisier, shouting "me, me, want me! Look at me!" The spiritual is quieter, whispering "Come."

If you set your mind on the material, it will take all your time and attention.

If you set your mind on the spiritual, you'll fill up on peace but still have plenty of room for the tinsel and the tree.

Enjoy the cookie. Make the great present. Just be sure that they do not become the point of the season, or the meaning of your life.

—EOR

A prayer for the season

Holy Spirit, when I become too caught up in material things, guide my eyes back to all that you are doing, for it is through you that I find life and peace. Amen.

JOY

ADVENT WEEK 3

THIRD SUNDAY

Imagine you're looking at a photo of God in the heavens. What do you see?

Clouds, check. Grey beard, sure.

Is God dancing? Is God laughing? Is God the perfect portrayal of pure contentment?

Sing your favorite song about God. What words does it use to describe God? My favorite today has these words: immortal, invisible, wise, mighty, victorious, hidden. Not a single word about God enjoying a good joke, or smiling at a kitten's Instagram antics.

You may think of God as huge, powerful, creative, and giving. But what about joyful?

We are taught to honor God by saying how big and glorious God is. We are taught to thank God for answered prayers or provision given. God is big, for sure, and able to do anything, so it's easy to picture the Divine Countenance as serious, even taciturn or grumpy. Does God's immensity and power that mean that God has to be a stick in the mud?

Scripture tells us that God enjoys the work of His hands. God enjoys His creation. God enjoys you.

With all that enjoying going on, God is surely joyful Himself.

When you think about a time when you were joyful, didn't God seem just a little closer than usual?

We get tired and angry, cynical and jaded. The labor of daily living can yank the joy right out of us.

But when you notice a flower springing from a sidewalk crack, that's God's joy you feel.

When you finish a difficult project and step back to enjoy your completion, that's God's joy in which you're participating. When a friend texts you out of the blue just to say hello, God's joy runs from celltower to celltower between you.

For God, existence itself is a joy. No wonder God is the source of our deepest joy. Joy simply overflows from God into us.

—EOR

Try this practice this week

Look for your moments of joy or contentment, and notice God in the midst.

THIRD MONDAY

I said in my prosperity, I shall never be moved... You had established me as a strong mountain. Then you hid your face; I was dismayed. To you, O Lord, I cried... Hear, O Lord, and be gracious to me, O Lord, be my helper! You have turned my mourning into dancing; you have taken off my sackcloth and clothed me with joy, so that my soul may praise you and not be silent. —Psalm 30

We've all been there, right? Riding along on your high horse, horizon in sight, plenty of green grass (for the horse) and caviar dreams (for you). And then: thud; oof. You hit the ground hard, wind's knocked out of you, the horse sees his chance and takes off.

Your losses didn't start with a horse, you say? I'm still guessing you know what the Psalmist was going through. He was feeling strong, successful, solid in his position, when suddenly everything fell apart. And because his life came crashing down he felt as though God's favoritism had vanished, taking everything good away too.

One of those times stands out for me. I had left my pastoring job, the farewell party was months behind me, and I was in Ohio for my doctoral program. I got a call from my denominational representative: I was to immediately cut contact with every person in my former church (i.e. remove them from my Facebook friends, cut them off my Twitter feed, disappear from social media) because the interim pastor felt threatened by me.

The call got uglier and increasingly bizarre and when I hung up I was alone, distraught, and tasked with cutting off others without a word.

I was in such a state that I accidentally threw away my grandmother's diamond earrings, which I had worn 24/7 for 20 years but had taken off because I'd lost the back of one.

Thud. Oof. Bye bye, horsey.

It took me years to stop crying out to God. But at some point I started experiencing joy again (mostly through singing) and in those moments when the hurt fell away and nothing stood between me and the Holy Spirit, all that mourning turned into dancing (or what passes for dancing when you're singing next to someone far better than you who doesn't dance).

That's how it is with joy and God. As Jesuit priest Pierre Teilhard de Chardin wrote "Joy is the infallible sign of the presence of God." As the Psalmist discovered, if you are joyful, God must be with you.

And when you are not joyful, and sorrow holds you fast, God is with you too. But it's easier to believe when you're content and at peace.

—EOR

When has your sorrow turned into joy? How long did it take you to realize that had happened?

THIRD TUESDAY

The pastures of the wilderness overflow, the hills gird themselves with joy, the meadows clothe themselves with flocks, the valleys deck themselves with grain, they shout and sing together for joy.   — Psalm 65:12-13

Remember Bob Ross? The fellow with the big fluffy hair who taught painting on PBS for a decade? Bob Ross is remembered for many things, but mostly for being very quiet and soothing, and for his "happy little trees." He'd be painting a landscape—a landscape in 30 minutes!—when he'd dab a different green paint onto the canvas, add some brown, and coo "let's build some happy little trees."

Ross's pleasure in creating shined through the tv screen, brighter than any LED or LCD or tube could show. When he added trees and clouds to a painting, the oils themselves seemed cheerful. (Don't think tubes of thick oil paint seem cheerful? You've been hanging with the wrong painters.)

More importantly, Ross created a safe space for creating.. His gentleness invited participation: "You can do anything you want. This is your world."

I imagine Bob Ross had more than a dab of God in him. Creating, inviting others to create too, finding beauty in the mundane: sounds like God to me. And you know how divine DNA is: can't really hide it when you are made in God's image.

Like Ross's, God's joy is contagious. God's joy is so captivating that the entire creation is filled with it. The hills gird themselves with joy. The meadows and valleys sing together for joy.

In God's world, joy is everywhere, from the happy little trees to the big fluffy clouds to meadows that clothe themselves with flocks and valleys that deck themselves with grain.

Flora and fauna become party clothes when God whips out a brush..

Today, see if you can slow down, just a bit. Notice how God's creation—the winds, the sky, the flowers, the snow—seem to dance and sing for joy. Then see if you can do the same. You are one of God's creations, after all.

—EOR

A prayer of thanks

Great artist, singer of happy melodies, my God: thank you, thank you. Fill me with your joy so that I can shout and sing with the meadows and the valleys, all those happy little trees and me.

THIRD WEDNESDAY

The wilderness and the dry land shall be glad, the desert shall rejoice and blossom; like the crocus it shall blossom abundantly, and rejoice with joy and singing....Strengthen the weak hands, and make firm the feeble knees, Say to those who are of a fearful heart, Be strong, do not fear! Here is your God. —Isaiah 35:1-4

Did you grow up with a scary second coming? More a threat than a promise?

That's not the way you're supposed to see it. Read through the Hebrew Bible and most of the Christian texts and you'll find a completely different view of the coming of the King. God shows up, causing happiness in the desert as it blossoms. The land itself rejoices, and God's people have plenty and peace.

God's coming is a promise of restoration and healing, the abundance of a Spirit-overflowing life.

That doesn't mean that we live fearlessly now, does it?

If you are growing older—and if you're reading this, you Are growing older—you have probably noticed changes in your body. Curves where they didn't used to be. New textures and colors, Greater skills but lesser strength.

Mortal things come into being, grow, age, and die, and because what's on the other side of bodily life isn't fully knowable we are deeply (if unconsciously) afraid of what death may bring.

Meanwhile, our sight grows dimmer (or at least less accurate) and we don't heal as quickly, so living also becomes a bit more tenuous, a shade more dangerous.

So when Isaiah evokes the splendor of creation upon the arrival of the coming King, he also counsels the people to "strengthen the weak hands, and make firm the feeble knees." He urges them to speak to their elders, as well as to others whose hearts are afraid, to be hopeful, to draw on their strength and speak back to their fear.

How can they be strong and not fear? A simple answer: Here is your God.

God's coming at Christmas scared King Herod enough that he murdered all the boy babies. Fear can make us foolish, or ugly.

If we are living well—reflectively, lovingly—we gain wisdom along with wrinkles. Joy sneaks stealthily into our lives as we mature spiritually. Joy rarely shouts its presence, but becomes part of who we are as we are filled with God and gratitude.

What can prevent the presence of joy is fear, for fear will fill every dark crevice of your mind if you allow it.

Fight fear if you would have joy.

—EOR

What fear stands in the way of your joy, or prevents you from seeing the glory of God, who is here?

THIRD THURSDAY

Sing for joy, O heavens, and exult, O earth; break forth, O mountains, into singing! For the Lord has comforted his people, and will have compassion on his suffering ones. But Zion said, The Lord has forsaken me, my Lord has forgotten me. Can a woman forget her nursing child, or show no compassion for the child of her womb? Even these may forget, yet I will not forget you. — Isaiah 49:13-15

If you're anything like me, the worst part of hard times is the terrible alliance between sorrow and abandonment. Your closest friend may be far, far away. Your own soul may seem to have withered with grief or pain.

You may feel alone and forgotten, even if people who love you are right there with you. Despair can grab hold of your heart, squeezing out sobs or draining it dry.

Your feelings are legitimate. That doesn't mean they accurately describe the whole of reality.

God is here, even now.

God never forgets. God's thoughts never wander. God's eyes are on you, and God's arms are always open to you. Like the perfect mother, God cherishes God's children, you among them, and wants nothing more than to draw them to Her divine bosom, holding them safe and warm.

That is the truth. It doesn't mean you're going to believe it. If you cannot act on it, you don't really believe it.

That says nothing about your faith or your relationship with God; it says everything about the power of despair.

You may not feel like God is near, so remind yourself of the truth: your closest friend is not the one at a distance. Your divine Friend is inside you and around you.

Remind yourself that no matter how you feel, your soul is cradled gently by a compassionate and loving God. You are not alone.

In your darkest moments, when the night sky fills every room, remember that the Light _has_ come. The worst darkness may hide light at times, but cannot overcome it.

—EOR

A prayer for the dark nights

Mothering God, I know you have not forgotten me but everything is dark and my spirit is restless. I cannot see you. Come to me as I cry out for you. I am lonely and scared and I need you. Have compassion, Mama, and comfort me. I want to sing for joy again, joining my voice with the mountains and the seas and all of creation.

> Though the fig tree does not blossom, and no fruit is on the vines; though the produce of the olive fails, and the fields yield no food; though the flock is cut off from the fold, and there is no herd in the stalls yet I will rejoice in the Lord; I will exult in the God of my salvation. —Habakkuk 3:17-18

It's easier to be happy when things are going your way. You have disposable income. Your friends text regularly. No troubling health issues. All you need is a bowl of ice cream and life feels good.

Happiness is a feeling, a fleeting emotion like all the others, dependent upon your environment, your body chemistry, and your momentary attitude. Happiness is not trustworthy. It's good, and you can enjoy it while it lasts, but don't aim for it. Chasing happiness is like looking for the next high: the chase itself is addictive and the crash on the other side devastates.

God is joyful—full of joy—because God cherishes and rejoices. God can see through the storms and fires and find satisfaction. God hears the mountains and the deserts singing, notices the one crocus peeking through snow, and smiles at the old people line dancing.

Joy is the result of the decision to notice the glorious around you, however small. Joy comes when you take full advantage of your capacity for wonder. Joy is inevitable when you hush your inclination to embarrassment and give in to your urge to dance in the grocery store.

I'm not saying it's easy. Lord knows, literally, I'm not saying it's easy. As someone who still gets embarrassed when I mispronounce a word or trip in the street: it's not easy.

You can choose joy. That's what gratitude journaling is about: turning your attention toward goodness and beauty.

God is the source of all goodness and beauty, so rejoicing in God is a good place to start.

Rejoice in the Lord today. Not because you have a roof over your head, if you do. Not because you have enough to eat, if you have. Not because your Christmas shopping is done, if it is.

Rejoice in the Lord today because when nothing is going your way, God is, and God will always give you strength to get through.

—EOR

How will you notice the glorious today?

Abide in me as I abide in you... As the Father has loved me, so I have loved you; abide in my love. If you keep my commandments, you will abide in my love, just as I have kept my Father's commandments and abide in his love. I have said these things to you so that my joy may be in you, and that your joy may be complete. And this is my commandment, that you love one another as I have loved you. —John 15, *excerpted*

I'm not very good at distinguishing between a demand and a desire. If my child says, "Would you bring me a glass of water?" it feels like a demand, even though I know she's just hoping I'll say yes.

I truly believe that God invites us, woos us, hangs out with us just because God wants to be with us and desires that we feel the same.

Have you ever had a friend or lover who just hangs out with you for no obvious reason? I'm the one who thinks "hmmm.... what does this person need or want from me right now?" rather than thinking (for example) "oh yay! This person wants to be with me!!!"

Yes, I do hear what I'm saying about myself. And maybe you.

So when Jesus says, "Abide in me... and your joy may be complete" I used to read that as "you'd better spend more time with Me and then maybe I'll give you some shred of happiness."

Or perhaps, "Here's what I demand: spend time with Me or else!!"

Those are my demon voices yelling falsehoods. Those voices sound so much like me that I take them seriously. Maybe you do too.

Jesus isn't laying down the law. Here's Jesus' guidance: I love you exactly as my Papa loves you; stick close to Papa and to me.It's a safe and loving place to be.

Invitation. No demand.

The only commandment Jesus gives here is this: love each other as deeply and thoroughly as I have loved you. Which is a pretty high standard, but way more do-able than "spend more and more time with Me or go to hell forever."

Jesus isn't demanding. He's just like the One he called Father. He wants to be with you, as does God: because They love you. Not because God's looking for an excuse to smite you.

There's only this: you can have with my Papa what I have; here's how. And what does Jesus have? Joy that is complete.

Sounds like a good trade to me.

—EOR

What's one thing you could do today to love just a little bit more?

LOVE

ADVENT WEEK 4

FOURTH SUNDAY

The Lord and his disciples entered the home of Martha. She had a sister named Mary, who sat down in front of the Lord and was listening to what he said. Martha was worried about all that had to be done. Finally, she went to Jesus and said, Lord, doesn't it bother you that my sister has left me to do all the work by myself? Tell her to come and help me! Jesus answered, Martha, Martha! You are worried and upset about so many things, but only one thing is necessary. Mary has chosen what is best. —Luke 10:38-42

As a recovering Martha it's taken me years to understand Jesus' point. After all, if you're the one who usually cleans and usually cooks and always remembers that medicine needs to be picked up at the pharmacy, Martha is your patron saint. If you're on her side of the mop, you know: Jesus gets to hang out in the living room chatting with his boys because someone's making sure he gets fed. And it's sure not Mary.

Jesus' problem with Martha isn't that she's finding food for the sudden arrival of a passel of men (one of whom is rumored to be the Messiah) instead of chilling at his feet.

Jesus may not like getting pulled into a sisterly squabble but he's managed siblings before (I'm looking at you, James and John).

Jesus gently chides Martha because he notices how she's feeling. Martha is worried, upset, anxious and overwhelmed and crabby. She could be lovingly preparing a very simple meal; she's not.

Hurry and multitasking are enemies of love.

The "best thing" Mary has chosen isn't listening to Jesus, and it isn't shirking work. Mary has chosen love. (And yes, it would have been awesome if she'd chosen love and set the table.)

We cannot love when we do not pay attention. We cannot love if worry and fear crowd our hearts.

In a season bent on showing people just how much you care about them through gifts and food, it's good to remember this:

Your beloveds want your presence more than your presents.

If you are feeling stressed over getting eighteen more details perfected by midnight on Christmas Eve, ask yourself: am I doing this to earn others' love (an impossible task, by the way)? Am I doing this for approval?

If it's either one, you're not doing it out of love.

Today: Stop. Breathe. Listen. Notice. Pray. Pay attention. And love, well.　　　　　—EOR

A prayer to try

Holy One, as I enter these last hours of Advent, help me to give up my perfectionism and my hustle. Quiet my guilt or worry or sadness or disappointment—anything that separates me from myself and from you. Guide me into doing the one thing that truly matters: accepting and giving love. Amen.

FOURTH MONDAY

For God so loved the world that he gave his only Son, so that everyone who believes in him may not perish but may have eternal life. Indeed, God did not send the Son into the world to condemn the world, but in order that the world might be saved through him.   —John 3:16-17

There is just one way to save the world.

The only way to save the world is through love.

Not sentimental love. Not hearts and lace and happy endings.

The only way to save the world is through love: God's love for each of us, and our God-enabled persistent choosing to act for the good of others.

That's what love is: willing the good of someone else and choosing to act for that good, even when it does not seem to benefit you.

God's love is like that: unwavering, unconditional, affection and care for every one of God's creatures, every atom of God's creation.

God's love is unwavering, unconditional, affection and care for you.

God acts on love by showing up, over and over again, with care and compassion, and selflessness, again and again.

Because you are worthy of rescue.

You. Are. Worthy.

And so is everyone else.

As you wait these last days for the child of God's love to show up, remember:

God loved you so much that God showed up in the flesh, knowing that anyone who trusts God's love will experience eternal living, now, in this material life.

—EOR

A prayer for God's love

Hopeful, peaceful, joyous, impossibly loving God: there is no one who gives so freely as you. I know that you chose to be human to show me exactly what real love is like. As I continue my Advent journey, and in the days and weeks and years ahead, please keep forming me to be like Jesus, recklessly loving all who pass my way. Amen.

FOURTH TUESDAY

My Father is glorified by this, that you bear much fruit and become my disciples. As the Father has loved me, so I have loved you; abide in my love ... I have said these things to you so that my joy may be in you, and that your joy may be complete.   —John 15:8-10

When God deals kindly with you, it's not because you do all the right things. You cannot do enough right things, or do things perfectly enough, to earn love. Anyone's love, but especially not God's.

Love isn't like that. Love cannot be earned. Love cannot be demanded.

You have no control over someone else's love.

That means that when someone loves you— truly wills your good and acts on it—it's because of who <u>they</u> are, not because of who you are.

When God loves you, it's because of who <u>God</u> is.

At the same time you cannot be enough to earn God's love there is a great mystery hovering over you:

You are enough for God.

With all your flaws, all your demon voices reminding you just how weak you are, with all your broken promises and failed project: you are enough for God.

You.

More mystery: When we are loved, and we accept that we are loved (which may be the hardest part), loving others is easier.

Your practice for today? Accept that you are loved.

And then live in that love, for love begets love. Just like God begat Jesus, love following love.

—EOR

A prayer for accepting and sharing love

Creating and loving God, there is nothing good that does not come from you, and the greatest thing that comes from you is love. You emanate love. All love comes from you. Help me to accept your love fully. Help me to live each day trusting you completely so that I am free to love others well, just as you do. Amen.

FOURTH WEDNESDAY

See what love the Father has given us, that we should be called children of God; and that is what we are...We know love by this, that he laid down his life for us—and we ought to lay down our lives for one another. How does God's love abide in anyone who has the world's goods and sees a brother or sister in need and yet refuses help? Little children, let us love, not in word or speech, but in truth and action. —1 John 3:1, 16-18

What does it mean to lay down your life for another person?

It's not about being a martyr. Have you ever known someone who didn't do what they wanted to do and always did what someone else wanted them to do? Not pretty, and not loving.

Laying down your life isn't about giving someone else what they want.

It's also not about dying in someone's place, no matter what you've been told.

Laying down your life means choosing to live in a different way than the way you are in the habit of living. You pick up your life as you know it and put it aside.

Laying down your life for another person means choosing to do things that aren't your favorites because doing them is good for someone else.

If you have ever had an infant living in your home, you have a sense of what laying down your life means.

The life you had before that baby came along was probably quite different than the one that included the child. You lay down your former life when the child showed up.

God could have remained on a lofty throne, doing what God does, risking nothing. That's not who God is. God chose to change what God was doing and get into the muck with us.

That is the kind of love that God has for us: a laying-down-the-life-you-expected kind of love.

That's the kind of love God wants us to have for others: a laying-down-the-life-you-expected-when-needed kind of love. And we're not expected to love only our own children, but God's children too.

Which is everybody. Including you, beloved child of God.

If you think of Jesus in that way—God laying down God's usual way of living so that we'd get to know God—he stops being a martyr we're supposed to emulate, and starts being a friend we get to appreciate.

—EOR

How are you loving in truth and action these days? What of your life are you willing to lay down if needed?

Beloved, let us love one another, because love is from God;
everyone who loves is born of God and knows God... for God
is love... and those who abide in love abide in God, and God
abides in them... There is no fear in love, but perfect love
casts out fear; for fear has to do with consequences, and
whoever fears has not reached perfection in love.

1 John 4, *excerpted*

Are you afraid of love? If we are honest with
ourselves most of us discover that we are
afraid of being loved or of loving, or both.

Loving requires us to act, to do things we don't
want to do.

Being loved can make us feel like we are in
perpetual debt that cannot be paid.

Being loved forces us to accept that we are
worthy of care, and to admit that we need care
more often than we would like to admit.

Yes, it could just be me.

We get scared of being disappointed, or of
disappointing others.

We get worried that if we do this loving action
we'll be committing ourselves to a hundred
more, and then what?

But when we are actually doing love—not
thinking about it, but doing it—fear goes away,
because God is in the actual loving.

We can love recklessly and indiscriminately
because God loves us so very very much.

God lived in this material, hurting world for just one reason: God loves and cherishes you.

God took on the pains and deprivations and joys and attractions and disappointments to show you how love is done.

Don't be afraid to love.

Try this: Spend two minutes in contemplation, eyes closed, mentally looking around for those people who truly love you. Not just the ones who say they love you, and not necessarily those who are the objects of your romantic affections. Notice the people in your life who are willing to do what they would not prefer to do, just because you are you.

Let the depth of their love touch your soul. If tears come, let them. If you get nervous, ride it out. Try to accept that in their eyes, you are beautiful and worthy of care.

And in God's eyes, you are even better than that.

—EOR

A prayer to try

Oh Mama God! Oh Papa! How you love me! I don't know what to do with that. I don't think I can even take it in. I'm afraid you're going to want something in return that I can't do. I'm afraid of disappointing you. Be patient with me (like you always are) while I try to soak up your love. Help me to pour it out as extravagantly as you do, for the sake of your world. Amen.

FOURTH FRIDAY ────────────

Hope does not disappoint us, because God's love has been poured into our hearts through the Holy Spirit that has been given to us. —Romans 5:5

Old Christmas movies are glutted with hope. Hope that Santa will come. Hope that she'll get the date with the guy. Hope that he'll have a tree that's more satisfying than a stick. Hope for a Red Rider BB Gun.

Those very same movies are also rife with disappointment as something hoped for goes wrong. No Santa, wrong guy, wrong present, until the lead character decides that hope and disappointment are too closely linked and so gives up hope.

An older British saying, known to the fans of John Cleese and Welsh soccer, is this: It's the hope that kills you.

Yet there's the Apostle Paul, writing to the persecuted Christians in Rome: Hope does not disappoint us.

Are these simply conflicting points of view? Paul the optimist vs every Christmas movie ever made? I don't think so. I think Paul knew something about hope that we tend to forget: hoping is not the same as wishing,

You can wish for anything, whether likely or outlandish. But actual hoping involves anticipating something you trust to happen, based on experience and reason.

You wish for a Red Ryder BB gun. You hope for a good breakfast after the opening of gifts.

Hope doesn't disappoint because it's based on trust and experience,

For Paul that experience includes God's love having proved trustworthy across generations and miles, and his own personal experience of God's love in his own heart.

We can hope without fear because we can trust Love.

Think you can't trust God's love? Ponder all the times you weren't hit by the car that ran the red light, including all the times you didn't even notice. Remember the food and shelter you *have* had, rather than fixating on what you haven't.

If Christmas passes without the gift you wanted or the guy you longed for or the tree that brushed the ceiling, remember that wishes don't always come true.

Love remains.

—EOR

Which of your hopes is really a wish?

If I give all I possess to the poor and give over my body to hardship... but do not have love, I gain nothing.
—1 Corinthians 13:3

Long before I was a pastor I worked at a church with massive and committed outreach to the poor and homeless in the city. From Thanksgiving through Christmas people who had more than we needed would bring blankets, clothes, coats, and sleeping bags, along with fanciful presents, to the church for distribution to thousands of people living in want or need.

There was a single rule about what could be given: The gifts had to be new. New blankets. New coats. New toys and books. Nothing used; only new.

At first I didn't understand this. "Look at how much more we could give if we accepted used things!" I wasn't alone in my puzzlement. Plenty of the organizations that took old things and redistributed them shook their heads.

One day I overheard the church's pastor explaining this policy to a potential donor. "Poor people always get used things. Hand-me-downs that don't really fit or have a small stain. Blankets that someone else didn't want. Even if what they hand down is in good shape, don't poor people deserve new things too?"

And then, "Don't you want to show them that they're loved as well as pitied?"

He wasn't saying that the used coat given out of love was worthless. If I had passed someone who needed a coat and I had one I wanted to give, he'd have been all for my handing it over.

The point was this: You can give everything to someone without really seeing them, without actually loving them.

You can work in the soup kitchen every week, give everything to Goodwill, hand out money to every guy standing on a traffic island, and do it all without any actual love, affection, attention, or kindness involved.

While it may bolster your pride and self-righteousness, and serve a good purpose, without love all your good works, all your carefully chosen presents, are as empty as your heart.

For God so loved the world…

Perhaps this Christmas, we can too.

—EOR

**Who needs to experience your love today?
How will you show it?**

CHRISTMAS EVE

What has come into being in him was life, and the life was the light of all people. The light shines in the darkness, and the darkness did not overcome it.... To all who did receive him, to those who believed in his name, he gave the right to become children of God—children born not of natural descent, nor of human decision or a man's will, but born of God. The Word became flesh and made his dwelling among us. We have seen his glory, as of a father's only son, full of grace and truth. —John 1

Reading the news reminds us that the world is a tragedy.

Starvation, military force, brutality, natural disaster, cruelty—all these seem intractable, as if ugliness were lodged in the very nature of human existence.

This is true: Darkness lodges itself in hearts, as well as in clouds of dust, shrapnel, and death.

This too is true: The light shines in the darkness, and the darkness has not overcome it. Over two thousand years ago someone we call John wrote down those three great truths: there is darkness, there is light, and the light is God in the world.

And, still, two thousand years later, the darkness has not, and can never, overcome the light.

During Advent we look toward tomorrow, both the calendar Christmas and tomorrow's promise of hope, peace, joy, and love.

Tonight let us remember that "the true light that gives light to everyone was coming into the world." And is, still.

—EOR

A prayer for Christmas Eve

Oh, Lord, how you must love us! Why else would leave your throne, give up power, eschew money, and become so vulnerable? Why else would you entrust yourself to our care? Only for love does anyone give up so much. Tonight, as we discover again the Christ child in the manger, let us also see the depth of your love in his face, and in all the other faces we encounter.
Amen.

CHRISTMAS

And Mary brought forth her firstborn son, and wrapped him in swaddling clothes, and laid him in a manger; because there was no room for them in the inn.

And there were in the same country shepherds abiding in the field, keeping watch over their flock by night. And, lo, the angel of the Lord came upon them, and the glory of the Lord shone round about them: and they were sore afraid. And the angel said unto them, Fear not: for, behold, I bring you good tidings of great joy, which shall be to all people. For unto you is born this day in the city of David a Savior, which is Christ the Lord. And this shall be a sign unto you; You shall find the babe wrapped in swaddling clothes, lying in a manger.

And suddenly there was with the angel a multitude of the heavenly host praising God, and saying, "Glory to God in the highest, and on earth peace, good will toward men."
—Luke 2:7-14 (KJV)

You know it, but it bears repeating.

That's the meaning of Christmas: God with us: Emmanuel.

May your heart be gladdened and your day bright with hope, peace, joy, and love.

But Mary treasured up all these things and pondered them in her heart. —Luke 2:19

I love the day after Christmas. It's when my (now-grown) kids and I wear our jammies all day, watch Marvel movies, eat leftovers and Xmas treats, and basically enjoy the afterglow of our favorite day of the year.

It comes after the long anticipation of Advent, the Christ-child's blessed arrival on Christmas Eve, and the joyous gift-swapping, overeating, and over-peopling of Christmas Day.

It's like a holiday from the holidays.

It's also the day when, if I'm quiet, I can feel the mystery of Christmas and the realness of real-life come together like no other day of the year.

I mean, even Mary stopped to reflect on all that had happened. Sometimes you just need a minute.

Fact is, the Jesus we celebrate ate leftovers. He spent time with those he loved doing nothing important. He liked a party. He probably would've enjoyed Black Panther.

The buildup to Christmas can be stressful, even exhausting. Even (especially) for those of us in ministry. So, if I may, let me encourage you today to rest, laugh, eat, nap, eat some more, watch a movie, read a book, enjoy your presents, or do whatever brings you joy.

Make December 26 a day you look forward to
every year. Your post-Xmas routine—and all
that goes along with it—will find you soon
enough.

—BKS

**What will you do today to rest your body, soul, mind, and
spirit?**

For the grace of God has appeared, bringing salvation to all, training us to renounce impiety and worldly passions, and in the present age to live lives that are self-controlled, upright, and godly, while we wait for the blessed hope and the manifestation of the glory of our great God and Savior, Jesus Christ. He it is who gave himself for us that he might redeem us from all iniquity and purify for himself a people of his own who are zealous for good deeds.   —Titus 2:11-14

"Self-control is the ability to regulate one's emotions, thoughts, and behaviors in the face of temptations and impulses." (Thanks, *Psychology Today*.)

As a teen, I chose to avoid secular (not-Christian) music, movies in theaters, and most parties and dances. My church said those things were bad for me, and I was a compliant kid who didn't question authority.

Every day I would read my Bible, practice piano (2 hrs), do 75 push-ups before bed, and keep my room tidy. I was self-disciplined at 16.

I was also afraid. And fear is a mighty strong motivator.

I wasn't afraid of my parents. And I wasn't afraid of my church. But I was afraid of God. Afraid that I'd make a misstep, fall into the enemy's snare, and be doomed to hell. That's a difficult tightrope to walk at any age.

Thankfully, I eventually outgrew those ideas about God—the petty, punitive God that I was afraid of.

But I'm not mad about all the self-discipline. It made me a more grounded, responsible teen—who could play a Joplin rag like nobody's business—and a more mindful, God-aware adult.

My motivations for living a self-controlled life now come from a desire to make life-giving choices rather than life-destroying ones. And I recognize that it takes more than just my will to do it.

I have to practice being patient, generous, others-centered, and the rest. But if I'm intentional about it, over time, I do become more like Jesus—"zealous for good deeds" as Paul puts it.

—BKS

How do you practice being like Jesus? What does self-control look like to you?

4TH DAY OF CHRISTMAS ───────

Simeon took him in his arms and praised God, saying,'
Master, now you are dismissing your servant in peace,
according to your word; for my eyes have seen your
salvation...'   —Luke 2:28-30

Simeon was old—like, really old—and the Holy Spirit promised him he wouldn't die until he saw the Messiah in the flesh. So this day, like most, he was at the Temple, eyes peeled, anticipating a Visitor. A king who would set Israel to right.

I don't know if Simeon expected the Promised One to show up as an infant. Certainly, the Jews weren't expecting their Messiah to arrive in swaddling clothes.

But when Mary and Joseph walked in carrying 40-day-old Jesus, the Holy Spirit tapped on Simeon's shoulder.

"This is him."

Simeon didn't miss a beat. He took the infant Emmanuel into his arms and gushed with praise for God. It was the culmination of his prayers, a fitting end to his (long) life's work, and the keeping of God's promise to him.

I'm sure there wasn't a dry eye in the place. Even Mary and Joseph were taken aback.

Not surprisingly, the Holy Spirit makes Jesus known to us too.

When we're hurting.

When we're tempted.

When we're lonely.

When we're broken.

Because Jesus came as a crying, messy Baby—
and grew up to become a Man of sorrows—he
can relate to the things we suffer. Even a
conquering King couldn't have done that.

—BKS

Where are you encountering Jesus?

> I will greatly rejoice in the LORD, my whole being shall exult in my God; for he has clothed me with the garments of salvation, he has covered me with the robe of righteousness, as a bridegroom decks himself with a garland, and as a bride adorns herself with her jewels. —Isaiah 61:10

Several years ago, I wrote a song called *Unreal*. In it, I admitted to feeling like I was the sum of my mistakes, like a consequence of my past choices, woefully missing the mark of God's expectations time and again.

I was nearing 40 at the time, beginning to come to terms with my sexuality, struggling with being a faithful husband, unsure of where I stood with God, and deeply depressed.

Being a successful Christian songwriter, an upstanding deacon in my Southern Baptist church, a proud Republican, and a super-nice guy were not enough to quiet what was going on in my head and heart. I might've fooled some, but God and I knew what was really happening.

When I looked in the mirror, I didn't see salvation or righteousness. I didn't have the confident swagger of a groom or the radiant beauty of a bride.

What I saw was brokenness, ugliness, and gut-level fear.

I wrestled with that lyric for weeks before arriving at a chorus that held out hope for me and for everyone who struggles with feeling unworthy:

You're so unreal, too good to be true
You and only You could bring me back to
life
It's so unreal how Your unrelenting grace
Flies into the face of everything I feel
The way You love is just unreal

I still feel unworthy sometimes. But the truth is
God loves and treasures me, clothing me in
salvation and righteousness. I don't always see
it, or feel it, but it's still true.

—BKS

**If you feel unworthy of God's love and acceptance, why do
you think that is? What are the ideas about God you have
that would need to change for you to feel worthy?**

6TH DAY OF CHRISTMAS ──────────

The Lord is not slow in keeping his promise, as some understand slowness. Instead he is patient with you, not wanting anyone to perish, but everyone to come to repentance. —2 Peter 3:9

There was a time when I was struggling in what felt like every area of my life. Nothing was working, and I didn't think I was making a difference anywhere, to anyone. I used to earnestly pray that God would give my life meaning.

I longed to know that I mattered, in that Kingdom kind of way.

That trying season continued for the longest time. I wondered why God wasn't opening a door somewhere, providing relief for my financial frustrations and giving me clear direction for my future.

I never stopped believing that God desired good things for me. But it seemed like God was moving at a glacial pace, if at all.

Meanwhile, I stewed and pouted and complained. Like a petulant kid waiting on his Parent to make everything better.

Somewhere in the midst of my mess, I read Jesus' words in John 16:33: "In this world you will have trouble. But take heart! I have overcome the world."

I began to understand that God didn't promise a life without trouble. God promised to be bigger than my trouble.

It isn't God's job to save me from the outcome of my choices. It is up to me to make different choices. I have to participate in my own overcoming.

A few years removed, I can look back and see that, even when I didn't realize it, God was working in and through my life for the good of the Kingdom, and for my good too.

—BKS

Have you been waiting for God to rescue you from your own choices? What could you be doing instead?

7TH DAY OF CHRISTMAS ———
NEW YEAR'S EVE

The LORD bless you and keep you; the LORD make his face to shine upon you, and be gracious to you; the LORD lift up his countenance upon you, and give you peace.
—Numbers 6:24-26

On New Year's Eve, most of us fall into one of two categories—those who feel the need to grieve what's passed, and those who need to celebrate and welcome what's coming.

This year, I'd like to propose that we be both.

Last year at my house, we wrote down things we wanted to say goodbye to before the clock struck twelve and burned them. I felt lighter after watching my breakup and Covid and various other pain-points go up in flames.

Did they go away? No.

Did it feel good to say "so long" to them before the ball dropped? Heck yes, it did.

Then we drank champagne and went to bed.

My point is this: there is room for both grieving and celebrating. We need both. Solomon knew that when he wrote in Ecclesiastes, "for everything there is a season." (3:1).

It's important to pay our respects—or at least attention—to the things that we're leaving behind. It's also important to say hello to the new that awaits with proper fanfare.

So…

Light a candle for someone, or something, you lost this year.

Say a prayer of thanks for lessons learned.

Acknowledge the healing that hasn't happened yet.

Call or write someone and make peace.

Forgive what—or who—you can.

All of it matters. A lot. Then…

Put on some funky music.

Pull out your party dress or cowboy hat or whatever makes you feel festive.

Dance in the kitchen.

Toast to possibilities.

Eat junk food.

Hug the people in the room, even if the only one there is you.

Then share the blessing God gave Moses to share with the Israelites with everyone you know. (It's at the top of the page.)

—BKS

What will you bid farewell this year, and what will you welcome?

NEW YEAR'S DAY

For everything there is a season, and a time for every matter under heaven.   —Ecclesiastes 3:1

"Happy New Year!!! Time to get to work! I want to lose ten pounds! I want $10K in my savings account! I'm gonna volunteer at the homeless shelter twice a month! I want to read a book a week! I'll call my mom twice a week! I'm gonna learn Mandarin, and winemaking, and sign language!"

-A Misguided, Overzealous Resolution-Maker

Yes, it's a new year. It's a time for restarts, refreshed motivations, and renewed perspectives. Something about turning the calendar year gets many of us really energized to accomplish and achieve. Nothing wrong with that.

But in my experience, New Year's resolutions—deciding to make a change or two (or twelve) in your life as the clock strikes midnight—result in more setbacks than successes.

Here's why: Just because I'm in a new year doesn't mean I haven't brought the old me along for the ride.

Changing those habits and behaviors takes a lot of difficult work. It requires a retraining of my mind—getting rid of negative attitudes and speaking back to demon voices of guilt and shame.

It demands a reshaping of my environment—adjusting what I watch, what I listen to, where I hang out and with whom.

And it means drawing close to God so that my sticky soul isn't drawn to the things I say I'd like to get away from.

I can't change anything significant about myself by an act of my will alone. The will just isn't strong enough.

So achieving a goal of $10K in the bank means looking at how I spend my money and why, as well as what I gain from saving—not just in material ways, but also how it benefits my emotional, mental, and spiritual health.

And that's before I do the work of creating a budget, living within it, and actually saving a buck or two.

—BKS

In Ecclesiastes, we read that there is a season for everything. Building, tearing down, dancing, weeping, feasting, fasting. Maybe this year, instead of making resolutions, start with the question, "What season am I in? What do I want the rest of this season to look like?"

Who is wise and understanding among you? Let them show it by their good life, by deeds done in the humility that comes from wisdom. But if you harbor bitter envy and selfish ambition in your hearts, do not boast about it or deny the truth. Such 'wisdom' does not come down from heaven but is earthly, unspiritual, demonic. For where you have envy and selfish ambition, there you find disorder and every evil practice.   —James 3:13-16

I used to have a successful career in the Christian music industry. I wore a lot of hats back then—publisher, record producer, studio musician—but the role that fit me best was always songwriter.

I was part of a tight-knit songwriting community in Nashville. My friends and I wrote many of the hits played on Christian radio back then. We celebrated one another's accomplishments. We made an impact on gospel music.

It felt good.

When I ostensibly left Christian music nearly 20 years ago, I also left behind that close camaraderie. I shed all the roles I'd played and shifted my creative focus to writing songs for me to sing. Songs that reflected my changing views on God, myself, and the world around me.

While I'm usually happy with the choice I made, I occasionally see where someone from my former peer group has had some success— a number-one single, a Dove Award nomination, or some other accolade—and I feel a twinge of "that used to be me."

I sometimes wonder, "What if I'd just kept writing those songs and nurturing those relationships? Am I not as talented as most of the Christian songwriters who are successful today?"

But then I remember a few important things.

I outgrew what I was writing. Those songs no longer felt honest or true to my experience of God.

If I'd let my career, ambition, or envy of others' success keep me there, it would've held me back from becoming who I am now.

Being a part of the Christian music status quo was not God's best for my life.

So I'd say I did the wise thing.

—BKS

When have you made a wise choice that ran against "earthly" wisdom? What happened?

He was in the world, and the world came into being through him; yet the world did not know him. He came to what was his own, and his own people did not accept him.
—John 1:10-11

Jesus was always a little ... different.

Stands to reason. But Jesus's differences didn't lead most people to believe he was the promised Son of God. Instead, he came off to most as odd, to some as delusional, and to everyone as, well, different.

His own people didn't see who he was. He didn't look or act like they thought a Messiah would. Instead of being a conquering hero, he was a thorn in the side of their leaders. He was controversial, counter-cultural. Some would say subversive.

And yet, there he was—God dwelling among them. Both human and divine.

I'd like to think I would recognize Jesus. But then, I suppose I rub elbows with him all the time.

That's because Jesus said that when we care for the poor, the sick, the beaten-down, the forgotten, the lonely, that we are, in fact, loving him.

So if we're looking for Jesus, we might just be looking in the wrong places. Like the Jews were then.

—BKS

Would you recognize Jesus? How?

11TH DAY OF CHRISTMAS ─────────

Now listen, you who say, 'Today or tomorrow we will go to this or that city, spend a year there, carry on business and make money.' Why, you do not even know what will happen tomorrow. What is your life? You are a mist that appears for a little while and then vanishes. Instead, you ought to say, 'If it is the Lord's will, we will live and do this or that.'
—James 4:13-15

When I was young, I had a Sunday school teacher, Mrs. Worrell, who would always add "If it be Thy will" to every prayer she prayed with us.

"Heal Sheryl of her allergies, if it be Thy will."

"Give safety to Dewayne Gill and his family as they travel to Florida, if it be Thy will."

I don't believe for a second that God wanted Sheryl to suffer with sniffles. Or for the Gills to break down on the interstate en route to Panama City. I don't think Mrs. Worrell believed that either. Still, in her prayers, she was offering deference to God, in the event that God wanted something different.

I want to defer to the will of God too—when I'm making plans, and when I'm asking God for something, for myself or for someone else.

But I don't believe God has a stake in whether or not I plan a trip to Hawaii in February, I assume that if it isn't to be, obstacles will start popping up and I'll change (or cancel) my plans accordingly.

Same goes for bigger things, like changing careers, starting a business, and moving across the country—all of which I did, not knowing for certain if it's what God desired for me at the time.

I used to be terrified of making a misstep that would result in God washing Their hands of me. But now I know that God is not that petty.

Instead of wringing my hands and worrying that God will be displeased with my choices, I spend time with God so that I have a pretty good sense of what They want for (and from) me. Then I do my best to act accordingly.

—BKS

Think about your life right now. What do you think God expects from you, and desires for you?

12TH DAY OF CHRISTMAS ———————

Do to others as you would have them do to you.
—Luke 6:31b

I remember when I was in kindergarten, my teachers would tell us to follow the Golden Rule. All the other rules—don't pull each other's hair, don't call each other names, don't take someone else's toy—all led back to that one Rule.

"Treat others the way you want to be treated."

What would our society be like if we all held up the Golden Rule as the standard—the expectation—for all our behavior?

I suppose if that were the case, and I were to encounter a houseless man on the street begging for money, I'd give him all the cash I had. I'd ask him if he was hungry and offer to provide him a meal. If he didn't have a safe place to sleep, I'd find him shelter, or offer him a bed at my house.

Because that's what I would hope someone would do for me.

If someone disagreed with me about the COVID vaccine, the climate crisis, women's rights, LGBTQ+ rights, immigration, or pretty much anything, I'd listen to their point-of-view. I'd approach their opinions with curiosity rather than judgment, and I wouldn't assume they were stupid or evil because their views differed from mine.

Because that's how I would hope someone would engage with me.

Following the Golden Rule is simple, but it isn't easy. Kindergarteners get it. Grownups get it too —we just add a bunch of caveats to it like it's a peace treaty or a bill stuck in Congress. Probably because it's just easier to put ourselves first.

But if we love our neighbors as we love ourselves, it makes for a way better time at the playground.

—BKS

Why do you think following the Golden Rule is so hard? What is one way you could practice loving your neighbor as yourself?